Dom's Handplant

Written by Judy Wilford
Photographed by Linda Bieniasz

Dom loved skateboarding, and he loved learning new stunts. But the only place where he could practice safely was the skateboard ramp, and that was a long way from home.

Every Saturday, Dom and his dad set off on the long trip to the ramp. They had to walk through the park, take a train to the city and then catch a bus.

 At the ramp, Dom met his friends. Together they put on their safety gear and talked about their favorite stunts.

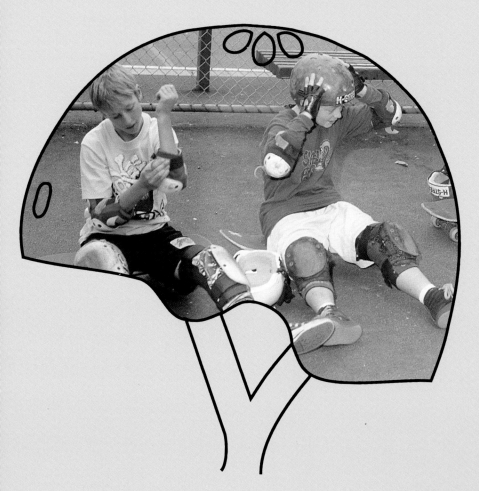

They couldn't wait to get onto the ramp.

Dom and his dad watched the other boys practicing while Dom waited his turn.

Dom's friends could do some amazing stunts. Sometimes they looked like they were flying through the air.

 Dom wondered if anyone would do the stunt that he was trying to learn. "No one's done a handplant yet, Dad," he said.

Then an older boy named Greg
had a turn on the ramp.
He did one of the best
handplants that Dom
had ever seen.

"Look!" Dom said to his dad. "That's
how you do a handplant. You have to
hold the board with one hand and tuck
your knees in. Then you have to plant
your hand on the edge of the ramp and
balance upside down."

Finally it was Dom's turn —
and naturally he tried to do
a handplant right away.

Tuck, plant and . . . oops!

He tried to copy Greg.

Tuck, plant and . . . he fell over again.

His arms were tired, but he still kept trying.

Tuck, plant . . . he *still* couldn't do it!

Dom wanted to keep trying.

But, as usual, it was soon time to go home.
Dom grumbled, "I wish the ramp wasn't so
far away. Then I could practice every day."

On the bus and the train Dom just stared
out the window.

"You must be tired," his dad said.

But Dom wasn't tired. He was thinking
very hard.

When they reached the park Dom said, "There are tennis courts in the park."

"Yes," said his dad.

"There's a playground and a picnic area."

"Yes?" said his dad.

"Well, why can't we have a skateboard ramp too?" said Dom.

"That's a good idea," said Dom's dad. "You should write to the mayor and suggest it!"

When Dom told his friends what his dad had said, they were very excited.

"A skateboard ramp's just what we want!" they said. "Let's all write letters to the mayor!"

So they did.

Dom waited days for the mayor to write back. Finally the letter came, and this is what it said:

CITY OF PINE HILL

OFFICE OF THE MAYOR

Dear Dominic,

Thank you for your letter suggesting that we should have a skateboard ramp in our park.

I am going to have a meeting to discuss the idea in more detail. I hope that you and your friends will be able to come.

The meeting will be held in the Pine Hill Town Hall on Monday at six o'clock.

I look forward to seeing you there.

Yours sincerely,

J. Johnson
Mayor of Pine Hill

On Monday, Dom and his friends
went to the Town Hall.

The meeting was held in a large room.

"Welcome," said the mayor, "We are here to talk about building a skateboard ramp in the Pine Hill park. I would like to know what you think."

A lady spoke first. She was worried about the children. "I think skateboarding is a dangerous sport," she said.

"No," said one of Dom's friends. "It's safer than it looks, and we have helmets, elbowpads, and kneepads to wear. Some of us have gloves, too."

Then a man said, "We have a beautiful park here in Pine Hill. I don't think we should cut down trees just to make a skateboard ramp."

"We won't have to," said Dom.
"There's a space next to the tennis courts.
We can leave all the trees."

The meeting went on for a little while
longer. Then the mayor said, "The next
thing I'll have to do is discuss it with the
council."

Dom shook the mayor's hand as he left.

"Thank you for having the meeting,"
he said.

This time Dom had to wait for weeks and weeks. He didn't know what the council had decided until he saw the headline in the local newspaper.

Weather Outlook:
Tuesday mainly fine with some cloudy periods in the afternoon.

PINE H

Printed and Published by Pi

Skatebo
to be Buil

The Pine Hill Mayor, Mr. Johnson, an today that a skateboard ramp will in the Pine Hill Park.

The Mayor said, "I believe that it is ve for us to look after the needs of Pine H Skateboarding is one of the most popular s children of today. By building our own giving them a place to skateboard safely. longer need to skateboard in the streets, long way from home to get to other r

"I have had a meeting with some who will be using the ramp. They have they take their sport very seriously an they will take good care of a ramp

parents have already

L NEWS

A full 7 day television guide inside. See page 14.

ress, 22 Station Street, Pine Hill.

rd Ramp
in Pine Hill

d
lt

ant
ren.
ong
are
ll no
vel a

ildren
e that
ve that
own.
to help
school.

They will be making sure that the children are wearing suitable safety gear."

The mayor said that builders will begin work on ill be built in the vacant area ill need to

Before long, people started building the skateboard ramp.

Dom went to the park every day after school to see what they were doing.

But he still went to the old skateboard ramp every Saturday. He wanted to get all the practice he could.

When the new ramp was finished,
Dom and his friends put on
a skateboarding demonstration.
Crowds of people came to watch.

Nick went first and everyone
started cheering.

 Then Pete whizzed up the ramp and did a perfect turn in midair.

The crowd cheered again.

One after another,
the boys did their
favorite stunts.

Dom watched nervously,
hoping that nothing
would go wrong
when it was his turn.

Finally Dom stood at the top of the ramp, determined not to make a mistake.

Then off he went.
Tuck, plant and . . .
The crowd began to cheer.

Dom did a perfect handplant!